THE WAY OF THE BUDDHA

EXPLORING THE LEGACY OF SIDDHARTHA GAUTAMA

DR. JAGADEESH PILLAI

Made with ♥ on the Notion Press Platform
www.notionpress.com

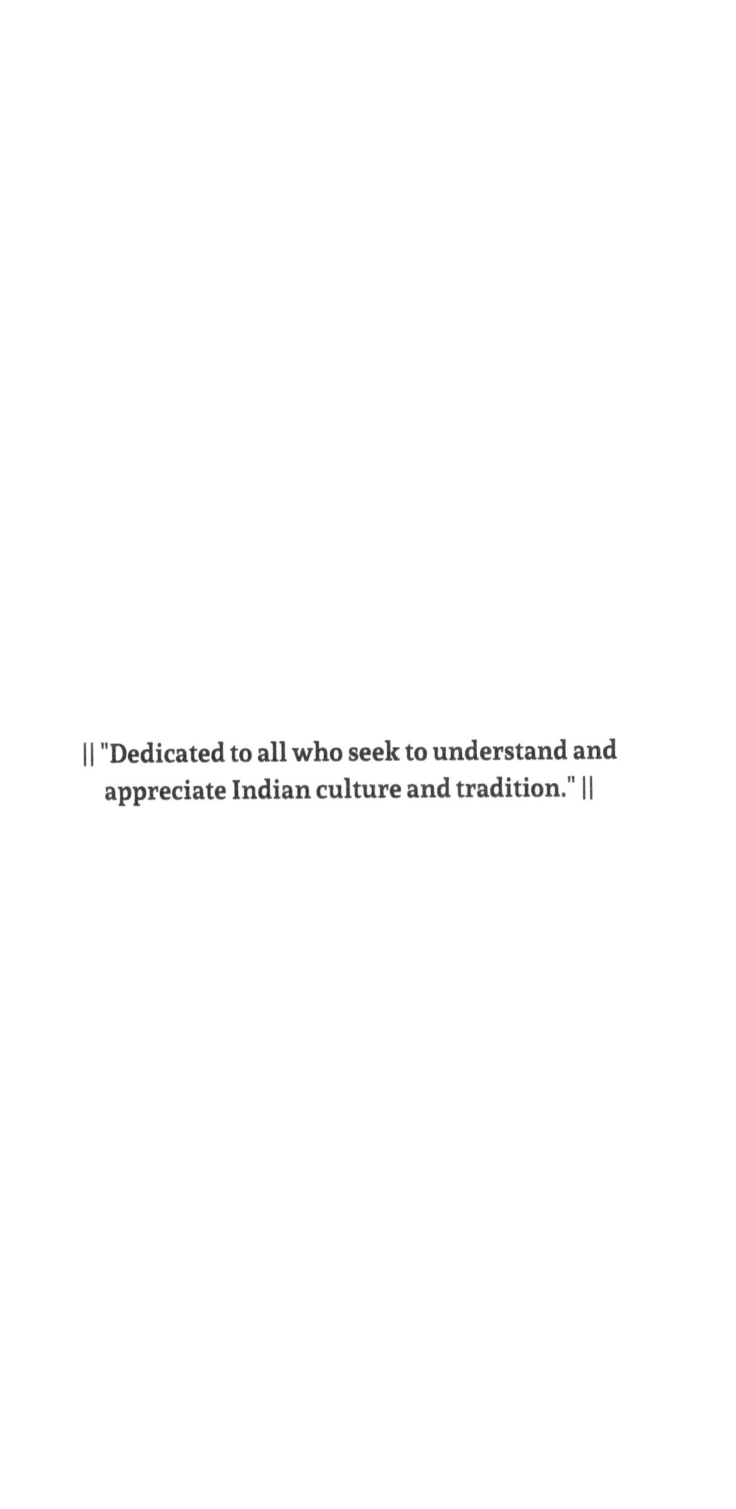

|| "Dedicated to all who seek to understand and appreciate Indian culture and tradition." ||

Contents

Contents

PRAYER

"Om Mani Padme Hum"

About The Author

Dr. Jagadeesh Pillai is a renowned Guinness World Record holder, writer, and researcher hailing from Varanasi, also known as the abode of Lord Shiva. With a Ph.D. in Vedic Science and a range of creative ideas and achievements, he is a true polymath. He is the author of more than 100 books including Research Publications. Although his roots can be traced back to Kerala, the people of Varanasi hold him in high regard and affectionately consider him one of their own.

Dr. Pillai has achieved four Guinness World Records in the following subjects:

"Script to Screen" - In this record, Dr. Pillai produced and directed an animation film within the shortest time possible, breaking the previous record set by Canadians. He has also received numerous national and international awards and recognitions for this achievement.

Longest Line of Postcards - For this record, Dr. Pillai created a line of 16,300 postcards on the occasion of the 163rd anniversary of Indian Postal Day. The event also included a questionnaire about the Indian flag.

Largest Poster Awareness Campaign - Dr. Pillai designed an awareness campaign on the subject of "Beti Bachao - Beti Padhao" (Save the Girl Child - Educate the Girl Child) to achieve this record.

Largest Envelope - In tribute to the Indian Prime Minister's

"Make in India" initiative, Dr. Pillai created a 4000 square meter envelope using waste paper to achieve this record.

Attempted - **70000 Candles on a 210 kg Cake** - To celebrate the 70th Indian Independence Day, Dr. Pillai attempted to light 70,000 candles on a 210 kg cake, which was recorded in World Records India.

Attempted - **Documentary on Dhamek Stupa of Sarnath in 17 Languages** - Dr. Pillai attempted to create a documentary on the Dhamek Stupa of Sarnath, dubbing it in 17 different languages. The result of this attempt is currently awaiting confirmation from the Guinness World Records.

Dr. Pillai is skilled in teaching the Bhagavad Gita, a Hindu scripture, and is popular among young people. He has helped many young people improve their lives through his motivational teachings.

In addition to teaching, he has composed and sung numerous Sanskrit Bhajans and patriotic songs.

He has also written and directed several short films and documentaries for awareness campaigns, and has volunteered with the police in both UP and Kerala to spread awareness about various issues through videos and photography.

Incredibly, he has produced and directed over 100 documentaries about the city of Varanasi, all on his own.

He has also helped and guided more than 25 boys and girls to achieve world records through creative and innovative methods. He is a multifaceted person who uses his intellect and the blessings given to him by God to excel in various areas. He is both a teacher and a student, always learning and teaching, and is able to master any subject he comes across.

He is a selfless social activist and motivational speaker who has overcome struggles and failures to become a successful and enthusiastic individual with a rich life experience.

In addition to his work with the Bhagavad Gita, he is also an efficient Tarot card reader, Astro-Vastu consultant, and a talented singer and composer. He has sung the entire Ram Charita Manas and Bhagavad Gita in his own compositions, and has sung the phrase "Lokah Samastha Sukhino Bhavantu" in 50 different languages. He is currently working on a detailed and scientific study of Vedas, Upanishads, Puranas, and the Bhagavad Gita. He has also composed and sung the Hanuman Chalisa and Gayatri Mantra in 108 and 1008 different compositions, respectively.

Awards - Four Times Guinness World Records, Winner of Mahatma Gandhi Vishwa Shanti Puraskar, Mahatma Gandhi Global Peace Ambassador, Kashi Ratna Award, Dr. APJ Abdul Kalam Motivational Person of the Year 2017, Mother Teresa Award, Indira Gandhi Priyadarshini Award, Bharat Vikas Ratna Award, Udyog Ratna Award, Vigyan Prasar Award, Poorvanchal Ratn Samman.

PREFACE

Siddhartha Gautama, most commonly referred to as the Buddha, was a wandering ascetic and religious teacher who lived in South Asia during the 6th or 5th century BCE and founded Buddhism. His teachings, which emphasize the Four Noble Truths, the Noble Eightfold Path, and the concept of karma, have had a profound impact on the world. This book, Buddha - Siddhartha Gautama, seeks to explore the life and teachings of the Buddha and their significance in the modern world.

This book is intended to serve as an introduction to the life and teachings of the Buddha for readers who are new to the subject. It explores the history of Siddhartha Gautama, the Four Noble Truths, the Noble Eightfold Path, and the concept of karma. The book also examines the impact of Buddhism on society and the global market, as well as its relationship to science and contemporary society.

The book draws on research from a variety of sources, including interviews with key figures in the Buddhist community, archival materials, and cultural analysis. I have also conducted extensive field research in South and Southeast Asia, including visiting Buddhist temples, interviewing monks and nuns, and attending meditation retreats. Through this research, I hope to provide readers with a comprehensive understanding of the life and teachings of the Buddha and their relevance to the modern world.

I am deeply passionate about the life and teachings of the

Buddha and hope that this book will help to spread the appreciation of this wonderful figure and his teachings. I believe that the Buddha has a great deal to offer to the world and I am excited to share his life and teachings with my readers.

I

Introduction to the Life and Teachings of the Buddha'

The life and teachings of the Buddha have been an important part of the religious, philosophical, and cultural landscape of Asia for over two thousand years. Siddhartha Gautama, known as the Buddha, is the founder of the Buddhist religion. Born in the 5th century BCE, Siddhartha was born into a wealthy family and had the opportunity to live a life of comfort and luxury. Despite his privileged upbringing, Siddhartha felt a deep sense of dissatisfaction with his life, and so he set out to find a solution to his problem. After leaving his family and embarking on a spiritual journey, he eventually reached enlightenment and became known as the Buddha.

The teachings of the Buddha are based on his realization of the Four Noble Truths and the Eightfold Path. The Four

Noble Truths are the core of the Buddhist teachings, and they describe the nature of suffering and the path to liberation. The first Noble Truth is that all life is suffering, or dukkha. The second Noble Truth is that the cause of this suffering is craving, or tanha. The third Noble Truth is that it is possible to end suffering, and the fourth Noble Truth is that this is accomplished by following the Eightfold Path. The Eightfold Path is composed of eight steps: Right Understanding, Right Thought, Right Speech, Right Action, Right Livelihood, Right Effort, Right Mindfulness, and Right Concentration.

The teachings of the Buddha are not only focused on liberation from suffering, but also on developing a compassionate and mindful life. The Buddha taught that all beings should aim to cultivate the five perfections of generosity, morality, patience, effort, and meditation. The Buddhist path of life centers around the practice of meditation, which is believed to bring greater understanding of the true nature of reality. Buddhism also emphasizes the importance of community and the need to foster loving relationships with family, friends, and society.

The life and teachings of the Buddha have had a profound impact on the spiritual and cultural development of Asia, and they are still a major source of inspiration and guidance for many people today. By following the teachings of the Buddha, people can find their own path to inner peace and liberation from suffering.

"The secret of health for both mind and body
is not to mourn for the past, worry about the
future, or anticipate troubles, but to live in
the present moment wisely and earnestly."
- Buddha

II

The Early Life of Siddhartha Gautama

Siddhartha Gautama, who later became known as the Buddha, was born into a wealthy family in what is now modern day Nepal, around the 5th century BCE. His father was a powerful ruler, and Siddhartha was brought up with privilege and luxury. Despite his comfortable lifestyle, Siddhartha was deeply unsatisfied with his life. He was deeply troubled by the suffering he saw around him, and he felt a strong urge to find a solution to this problem.

At the age of 29, Siddhartha decided to leave his family and embark on a spiritual journey in search of a solution to this problem. After several years of ascetic practices, he eventually reached enlightenment and became known as the Buddha.

The teachings of the Buddha are based on his realization of the Four Noble Truths and the Eightfold Path. According to these teachings, the cause of suffering is craving and the way to end suffering is to follow the Eightfold Path. The Eightfold Path is composed of eight steps: Right Understanding, Right Thought, Right Speech, Right Action, Right Livelihood, Right Effort, Right Mindfulness, and Right Concentration.

The teachings of the Buddha also emphasize the importance of living a compassionate and mindful life. The Buddha taught that all beings should aim to cultivate the five perfections of generosity, morality, patience, effort, and meditation. Buddhism also stresses the need to foster loving relationships with family, friends, and society.

The life and teachings of the Buddha have been an important part of the religious, philosophical, and cultural landscape of Asia for over two thousand years. By following his teachings, people can find their own path to inner peace and liberation from suffering.

"Holding on to anger is like grasping a hot
coal with the intent of throwing it at someone
else; you are the one who gets burned."
- Buddha

ॐ

III

The Four Noble Truths

The Four Noble Truths are the core of the Buddhist teachings, and they describe the nature of suffering and the path to liberation.

The four truths are:

1) life is suffering (dukkha);

2) the cause of suffering is craving (tanha);

3) it is possible to end suffering; and

4) this is accomplished by following the Eightfold Path.

The Eightfold Path is composed of eight steps:

Right Understanding,

Right Thought,

Right Speech,

Right Action,

Right Livelihood,

Right Effort,

Right Mindfulness, and

Right Concentration

By recognizing the Four Noble Truths and following the Eightfold Path, a person could find release from craving and attachment to the things of the world and liberate oneself from the endless cycle of suffering experienced through rebirth and death.

ॐ

"You will not be punished for your anger, you
will be punished by your anger."
- Buddha

ॐ

IV

The Noble Eightfold Path

The Noble Eightfold Path is the fourth of the Four Noble Truths in Buddhism, and is considered to be the path to liberation from suffering.

The eight steps of the Noble Eightfold Path are: **Right View, Right Resolve, Right Speech, Right Conduct, Right Livelihood, Right Effort, Right Mindfulness, and Right Concentration.**

These eight steps are often grouped together under their broader categories: **Integrity, Focus, and Wisdom.**

Right View is the knowledge of the Four Noble Truths.

Right Resolve is to be resolved on renunciation—the wish to be freed from suffering, resolved on freedom from ill-will, and resolved on harmlessness.

Right Speech is avoiding lies, malicious talk, harsh words, and idle chatter.

Right Conduct is abstaining from killing, stealing, wrong sexual behavior, and intoxicants.

Right Livelihood is refraining from wrong occupations.

Right Effort is the effort to abandon wrong thoughts and cultivate virtuous thoughts.

Right Mindfulness is the awareness of the body, feelings, mind, and mental objects.

Right Concentration is the practice of meditation.

"The only real failure in life is not to be true
to the best one knows."
- Buddha

V

Karma and Rebirth

Karma and rebirth are two of the most important concepts in Buddhism, and they are both intertwined in Buddhist teachings. Karma is the law of cause and effect, which states that all actions have consequences and all actions have a cause. It is believed that karma creates our life circumstances, and that each person is responsible for their own karma and the resulting life experiences that come from it. Karma and rebirth are related in that the consequences of our actions have an effect on our future lives, and what we do in this life will affect our future lives.

Rebirth, in Buddhism, is the belief that after death, a person is reborn into a new body and life, determined by the karma they have accumulated throughout their past lives. It is believed that each person has an inexhaustible store of karma that they must work through in order to achieve nirvana, which is a state of perfect peace. The only way to escape this cycle of death and rebirth is to become enlightened, and to do this a person must live a life of compassion, kindness, and morality.

Karma and rebirth are two of the most foundational Buddhist teachings, and they are intertwined in many ways. Karma is the cause, and rebirth is the effect. It is believed that the consequences of our actions in this life will affect our future lives in the form of karma, and that the karma we accumulate will determine our future rebirths. Karma and rebirth are both fundamental to Buddhist teachings, and they are both seen as essential to the process of achieving enlightenment.

Karma and rebirth are both seen as necessary in order to achieve enlightenment and nirvana. Karma is the cause and rebirth is the effect, and it is believed that by understanding and working through the karma we accumulate in this life, we can eventually achieve liberation from the cycle of death and rebirth and escape the suffering associated with it. It is through this understanding that Buddhism teaches us to live our lives with compassion, kindness, and morality, in order to accumulate good karma and achieve liberation.

"The way is not in the sky. The way is in the heart."
- Buddha

ॐ

VI

The Significance of Meditation

Meditation is an important part of Buddhist practice, and it is used to cultivate mindfulness and awareness. Meditation is seen as a way to quiet the mind and become more aware of one's thoughts, feelings, and emotions. This allows us to become less reactive to our environment and more aware of our own inner experience.

The goal of meditation in Buddhism is to develop insight and understanding into the nature of reality and the nature of our own minds. Through the practice of meditation, we can come to understand the impermanence of all things and the interconnectedness of all experience. This understanding can lead to a greater sense of peace and well-being, as well as a greater sense of compassion and understanding for ourselves and others.

Meditation can also help us to cultivate virtues such as

patience, kindness, and compassion. Through the practice of meditation, we can become more aware of our own thoughts and reactions, allowing us to choose how to respond more skillfully. This can help us to cultivate a more patient attitude towards ourselves and others, as well as a more compassionate attitude towards all of life's experiences.

Meditation can also help us to become more mindful of our own actions and the consequences of our actions. This can help us to make better decisions and lead a more ethical and moral life, as well as to become more aware of the effects our actions have on ourselves and others.

Meditation is an important part of Buddhist practice, and it can help us to become more aware of our thoughts, feelings, and emotions. It can help us to cultivate virtues such as patience, kindness, and compassion, as well as to become more mindful of our own actions and their consequences. Through the practice of meditation, we can come to understand the impermanence of all things and the interconnectedness of all experience, leading to a greater sense of peace and well-being.

"Your work is to discover your work and then with all your heart to give yourself to it."
- Buddha

VII

The Impact of Buddhism on Society

Buddhism is one of the world's oldest religions, and it has had a profound impact on many societies across the globe. Buddhism has shaped the cultures, religions, and philosophies of many countries and regions, and it has influenced the way people live their lives in various ways.

One of the most important impacts of Buddhism on society is the concept of karma. Karma is the idea that our actions have consequences, and that these consequences will follow us through our lives and into our future lives. This concept has been adopted by many religions and cultures, and it has been used to promote morality and ethical behavior.

Another impact of Buddhism on society is the concept of

mindfulness. Mindfulness is the practice of being present and aware of one's thoughts, feelings, and actions. This practice has been adopted by many cultures, and it has been used to promote psychological well-being and improved mental health.

Buddhism has also had a profound impact on the political and social structures of many societies. It has been used to promote social justice and equality, and it has been used to oppose the caste system and other oppressive structures. It has also been used to promote peace and non-violence, and it has been used to oppose war and conflict.

Buddhism has also had a profound impact on many countries' cultures and art. It has been used to promote literature, art, music, and poetry, and it has been used to promote spiritual and religious practices. It has also been used to promote education and scientific pursuits, and it has been used to promote philosophical inquiry and debate.

Buddhism has had a profound impact on many societies across the globe. It has shaped cultures, religions, and philosophies, and it has influenced the way people live their lives in various ways. It has been used to promote morality and ethical behavior, mindfulness and psychological well-being, social justice and equality, peace and non-violence, and literature, art, music, and poetry. It has also been used to promote education and scientific pursuits, and it has been used to promote philosophical inquiry and debate.

"Peace comes from within. Do not seek it without."
- Buddha

VIII

Buddhism and the Global Market

Buddhism and the global market have had a long and intertwined history. Buddhism has been a part of the global market since the days of the Silk Road, when merchants and traders brought goods and ideas from East to West. As trade increased and expanded, Buddhism spread to new areas and had an influence on the global market.

Buddhism has had a positive impact on the global market by promoting ethical behavior and morality. It has been used to promote fairness and justice in international trade, and it has been used to oppose exploitation and unfair labor practices. It has also been used to promote sustainable economic development, and it has been used to promote respect for the environment and natural resources.

Buddhism has also been used to promote a more mindful approach to business. Many Buddhist teachings emphasize the importance of personal responsibility and self-awareness, and this can be applied to business practices. For example, Buddhist teachings can be used to promote ethical decision-making and responsible consumption, as well as to encourage a more mindful approach to the use of resources and the production of goods.

Buddhism has also had an impact on the global market in terms of design and marketing. Buddhist-inspired designs and concepts have been used to create products and services that appeal to a global audience. For example, Buddhist-inspired designs are often used to create clothing and other items that are marketed as "mindful" or "spiritual."

Buddhism has had a long and intertwined history with the global market. It has been used to promote ethical behavior and morality, as well as to promote a more mindful approach to business. It has also been used to promote sustainable economic development and to oppose exploitation and unfair labor practices. Additionally, Buddhist-inspired designs and concepts have been used to create products and services that appeal to a global audience.

"It is better to conquer yourself than to win a
thousand battles."
- Buddha

IX

The Legacy of Siddhartha Gautama

Siddhartha Gautama, better known as the Buddha, is one of the most influential figures in world history. He is credited with founding the Buddhist religion, which has adherents all over the world. The teachings of the Buddha have had a profound impact on the world, and they continue to shape our lives and the way we think today.

The legacy of the Buddha is rooted in his teachings on the Four Noble Truths and the Eightfold Path. These teachings provide a framework for understanding the human condition and finding a path to liberation from suffering. The Four Noble Truths are the truth of suffering, the truth of the cause of suffering, the truth of the end of suffering, and the truth of the path that leads to the end of suffering. The Eightfold Path is the path that leads to the end of suffering and includes right understanding, right intention, right speech, right action, right livelihood, right effort, right mindfulness, and right concentration.

The teachings of the Buddha have also had a profound impact on the way we think about the world and our place in it. Buddhism emphasizes the importance of understanding the interconnectedness of all things, the impermanence of all things, and the importance of letting go of attachment and desire. All of these teachings have been influential in shaping our understanding of the world and our relationship to it.

The legacy of the Buddha is also rooted in his influence on the way we lead our lives. The Buddha taught the importance of leading an ethical life, of being mindful and aware of our thoughts, feelings, and actions, and of cultivating virtues such as kindness, patience, and compassion. His teachings have been used to promote mental health and psychological well-being, and they have been influential in the development of modern psychology.

The legacy of Siddhartha Gautama, better known as the Buddha, is one of the most profound and influential legacies in world history. His teachings on the Four Noble Truths and the Eightfold Path provide a framework for understanding the human condition and for finding a path to liberation from suffering. His teachings have also been influential in the way we think about the world and our place in it, and they have been used to promote mental health and psychological well-being. His influence on the way we lead our lives has been profound, and his teachings continue to shape our lives and the way we think today.

"You can search throughout the entire universe for someone who is more deserving of your love and affection than you are yourself, and that person is not to be found anywhere."
- Buddha.

X
Buddhism and Science

Buddhism and science are two different but complementary approaches to understanding the world. While science seeks to explain the physical world through empirical observation and experimentation, Buddhism seeks to understand the mental and spiritual realms through contemplation and meditation. Despite their differences, both Buddhism and science have the same goal of understanding the world, and they often find common ground in areas such as neuroscience, psychology, and philosophy.

One example of the common ground between Buddhism and science is the concept of mindfulness. Mindfulness is the practice of observing one's thoughts and emotions without judgment. It is often practiced in Buddhist meditation, and it has also been studied extensively by modern science. Studies have found that mindfulness can reduce stress, improve mental clarity, and promote overall well-being.

Another example of the common ground between Buddhism and science is the concept of the "mind-body connection". Both Buddhism and science recognize the importance of understanding how our mental and physical states are interconnected. Studies have found that mental states such as stress, anxiety, and depression can have a negative effect on physical health, and that physical health can influence our mental states.

Buddhism and science also find common ground in the area of neuroscience. The Buddhist concept of "mindfulness" can be studied using modern neuroscientific techniques such as functional magnetic resonance imaging (fMRI). Studies have found that mindfulness can have a positive effect on the brain, and that it can even help to reverse the effects of age-related cognitive decline.

Finally, Buddhism and science have also begun to find common ground in the area of philosophy. Buddhist philosophy is founded on the idea that the ultimate nature of reality is emptiness, or non-self. This idea is similar to the scientific concept of emergence, which states that complex systems can arise out of simple components. This common ground has been explored in depth by philosophers such as Alan Wallace and Evan Thompson.

Buddhism and science have both sought to understand the world in different ways, but they often find common ground in areas such as neuroscience, psychology, and philosophy. In the future, Buddhism and science are likely to continue to find common ground as they explore new areas of understanding.

*"Drop by drop is the water pot filled.
Likewise, the wise man, gathering it little by
little, fills himself with good."*

૭૩

XI

Buddhism and Contemporary Society

The relationship between Buddhism and contemporary society is complex. Buddhism is a religion and philosophy that originated in India more than 2,500 years ago and has since spread to countries around the world. In today's world, Buddhism is practiced by more than 500 million people, making it one of the largest religions in the world.

Buddhism has had a profound influence on contemporary society. Its teachings on the Four Noble Truths and the Eightfold Path have shaped our understanding of the human condition and provided a framework for finding a path to liberation from suffering. Buddhism's emphasis on understanding the interconnectedness of all things and the importance of letting go of attachment and desire have also been influential in shaping our understanding of the world and our relationship to it.

The Buddhist emphasis on ethics and morality has also had a major impact on contemporary society. Buddhist teachings on the need to lead an ethical life and cultivate virtues such as kindness, patience, and compassion have been influential in the development of modern psychology and in the promotion of mental health and psychological well-being.

In addition, Buddhism has also had a major influence on the way we lead our lives. Buddhism encourages us to be mindful and aware of our thoughts, feelings, and actions, and to practice meditation and contemplation in order to gain insight into the nature of reality. This has led to the development of new forms of meditation such as mindfulness meditation, which has become popular in the West.

Finally, Buddhism has also had an impact on the way we think about the world and our place in it. Buddhism's emphasis on understanding the interconnectedness of all things and the impermanence of all things has been influential in promoting global understanding and cooperation. Buddhism's teachings on compassion and understanding have also been influential in promoting world peace and world justice.

Buddhism has had a profound influence on contemporary society. Its teachings on the Four Noble Truths and the Eightfold Path have shaped our understanding of the human condition and provided a framework for finding a path to liberation from suffering. Its emphasis on ethics, morality, and mindfulness have been influential in the development of modern psychology and in the promotion of mental health and psychological well-being. Buddhism's teachings on the interconnectedness of all things and the impermanence of all things have also been influential in promoting global understanding and cooperation, and in promoting world peace and world justice.

"Let none find fault with others; let none see
the omissions and commissions of others. But
let one see one's own acts, done and undone."

ॐ

OTHER BOOKS OF THE AUTHOR

1. The Moments When I Met God
2. Kashiyile Theertha Pathangal
3. GURU GYAN VANI
4. Abhiprerak Gita
5. ASSI SE JAIN GHAT TAK
6. Hopelessness of Arjuna
7. The Soul and It's True Nature
8. Sense of Action (Karma)
9. Action through Wisdom
10. Action through Wisdom
11. THEORY AND PRACTICAL OF EVERY ACTION
12. LOGICAL UNDERSTANDING OF THE SUPREME
13. THE IMPERISHABLE SUPREME
14. Yatra Nishadraj se Hanuman Ghat Tak
15. Yatra Karnatak Ghat se Raja Ghat Tak
16. Yatra Pandey Ghat se Prayagraj Ghat Tak
17. Yatra Ranjendra Prasad Ghat se Dattatreya Ghat Tak
18. YaatraSindhiya Ghat se Gwaliar Ghat Tak
19. Yatra Mangala Gauri Ghat se Hanuman Gadhi Ghat Tak
20. Yatra Gaay Ghat Se Nishad Ghat Tak
21. MAA GANGA, GHATEN EVM UTSAV
22. Ganga Arti Dev Deepavali evam Any Utsav
23. Potentials of Digitalized India
24. VEDIC CONSCIOUSNESS
25. A Brief Introduction to Vedic Science
26. Kashi ke Barah Jyotirling
27. IMPACT OF MOTIVATION
28. Let's have a Milky Way Journey
29. Color Therapy in a Nutshell

30. Rigveda in a Nutshell
31. Yajurveda in a Nutshell
32. Samveda in a Nutshell
33. Atharva Veda in a Nutshell
34. Ayushman Bhava - Ayurveda
35. Srimad Bhagavad Gita and Upanishad Connection
36. Srimad Bhagavad Gita - an attempt to summarize each chapter.
37. Facts and Impact of Nakshatra
38. Astro Gems - NAVARATNA
39. Ekadashi - A Concise Overview
40. A Concise View of Hanuman Chalisa
41. Inspirational Gita
42. Nakshatraranyam
43. Summary of 18 Mahapuranas
44. Synopsis of 18 Upa Puranas
45. Rigvediya Upanishads
46. Shukla Yajurvediya Upanishads
47. Krishna Yajurvediya Upanishads
48. Samavediya Upanishads
49. Atharvavediya Upanishads
50. The Seven Great Sages
51. From Rocket Scientist to President Dr. APJ Abdul Kalam
52. The Visionary's Voice - Quotes of Dr. APJ Abdul Kalam
53. The Wisdom of Swami Vivekananda: Insights and Inspiration from a Legendary Spiritual Teacher
54. Ayurvedic Remedies from the Garden
55. Sages and Seers
56. Rising Strong – Motivational Stories of Women
57. Beyond Flames -Mystery stories of Funeral Ghat Manikarnika
58. The Origins of Tulsi: A Look at the Mythological Roots of the Plant"

59. The Holistic Cow: A Look at the Physical, Spiritual, and Cultural Importance of Cows in India
60. Arts of Healing
61. Exploring the Divine
62. Understanding Five Elements
63. The Etymology of Ram
64. Symbols of India
65. Voice of Change (About Speeches of Great Men)
66. She Speaks (About Speeches of Great Women)
67. Patriotism on Celluloid – Brief About Patriotic Films
68. The Music of Motivation: A Brief Guide to Inspirational Film Songs
69. Unlocking the Secrets of the Dashopanishads
70. A Cultural Mosaic
71. Ancient Traditions, Modern Minds
72. Ecos of Ancient Wisdom
73. Beneath the Surface
74. From Temples to Ashrams
75. Sages of the Subcontinent
76. The Art of Healling (Ayurveda, Yoga & Naturopathy)
77. Indian Kitchen
78. The Festivals of India
79. The Indian Epics Retold
80. The Power of Mantras
81. The Indian River Ganges
82. The Indian Architecture
83. Rites of Passage
84. The Indian Silk Road
85. The Indian Literature
86. The Indian Villages
87. The Indian Folks & Crafts

CONTACT

DR. JAGADEESH PILLAI

PhD in Vedic Science

Four Times Guinness World Record Holder

Winner of Mahatma Gandhi Vishwa Shanti Puraskar and
Global Peace Ambassador

Gemology, Astro & Vastu Consultant - Spiritual Counselor

Consultant for designing World Record Ideas

Efficient Tarot Card Reader

9839093003

myrichindia@gmail.com

drjagadeeshpillai@facebook

drjagadeeshpillai@instagram

jagadeeshpillai@youtube

www. JAGADEESHPILLAI.com

|| LOKAHA SAMASTHAHA SUKHINO BHAVANTU ||

• 57 •